T0054049

First published in 2020
by Jessica Kingsley Publishers
73 Collier Street
London N1 9BE, UK
and
400 Market Street, Suite 400
Philadelphia, PA 19106, USA

www.jkp.com

Copyright © Debby Elley and Tori Houghton 2020
Illustrations copyright © J.C. Perry 2020

All rights reserved. No part of this publication may be reproduced in any material form (including photocopying, storing in any medium by electronic means or transmitting) without the written permission of the copyright owner except in accordance with the provisions of the law or under terms of a licence issued in the UK by the Copyright Licensing Agency Ltd. www. cla.co.uk or in overseas territories by the relevant reproduction rights organisation, for details see www.ifrro.org. Applications for the copyright owner's written permission to reproduce any part of this publication should be addressed to the publisher.

Warning: The doing of an unauthorised act in relation to a copyright work may result in both a civil claim for damages and criminal prosecution.

Library of Congress Cataloging in Publication Data
A CIP catalog record for this book is available from the Library of Congress

British Library Cataloguing in Publication Data
A CIP catalogue record for this book is available from the British Library

ISBN 978 1 78775 380 8
eISBN 978 1 78775 381 5

Printed and bound in China

The Ice-Cream Sundae Guide to Autism

An Interactive Kids' Book for Understanding Autism

Debby Elley and Tori Houghton
Illustrated by J.C. Perry

Jessica Kingsley Publishers
London and Philadelphia

SUNDAE GLASS: PERSONALITY

Autism is just like an ice-cream sundae. There are lots of ingredients that go into it.

But before we start creating an ice-cream sundae, we need a sundae glass.

There are so many types of sundae glasses. Some are plain and simple, some are loud and proud! In fact, sundae glasses are just like people – we're all different.

Because we all have different personalities, autism doesn't look the same in everybody.

THE ICE-CREAM SUNDAE: THREE THINGS IN COMMON

The main ingredient in any ice-cream sundae is ice cream itself!

You may have heard of a Neapolitan ice cream.

It has three flavours: chocolate, vanilla and strawberry.

YUM!

These flavours are just like the three things that all autistic people have in common.

We'll tell you about those in a moment.

DIFFERENT-SIZED SCOOPS

The scoops of ice cream can be different sizes in a sundae, can't they?

And guess what? In our autism sundae it's the same, because autism is different in everyone.

It's true, we all have different personalities.

And if you're autistic, you'll have different amounts of 'autism' ingredients, too. Your own special mix.

Let's see what goes into our ice-cream sundae!

CHOCOLATE ICE CREAM: TROUBLE WITH WORDS

Let's start with the chocolate scoop!

Everyone on the autism spectrum has some trouble with words or what some people call 'speech and language'.

We can show this in our picture with a scoop of chocolate ice cream.

Some children on the autism spectrum don't speak at all, but they may learn to use sign language and pictures instead. They may learn to talk when they are a bit older – some do, and some don't.

Some children on the autism spectrum can speak. They may need extra help knowing what to say and how to say it.

ICE-CREAM SPOON: HELPFUL PEOPLE

Our ice-cream scoops show the main things that people on the autism spectrum can find difficult. The good news is that, with some help, those things can get easier. It's just like using a spoon to make the ice-cream scoops smaller!

If someone has trouble with words, a person called a speech and language therapist, or a speech and language pathologist, may help at home or at school.

Look at the spoon in this picture – just like a speech and language therapist, it is making our ice-cream scoop smaller!

When you see the spoon symbol in this book, it means we have shared some ideas that friends and family can use to help a person on the autism spectrum.

UNDERSTANDING WORDS

When we talk to other people, there are two things that we do.

We speak and we listen.

A bit like a computer, some brains understand words and their meanings extremely quickly.

Many people on the autism spectrum are good at talking, but they can find it hard to listen and understand clearly what is being said to them. Words can seem to whizz around too fast!

Autistic brains can be slower at understanding words or what we call 'processing' them.

If you are on the autism spectrum, the chances are that you find it easier to LOOK at words and pictures than to LISTEN to lots of information.

When you see the chocolate scoop, think of all the things you find tricky about words.

Other people can help by speaking at the right speed for the person who is listening, or by showing them pictures if they don't quite understand the words.

EVERYDAY PHRASES

Lots of people on the autism spectrum can speak but have difficulty understanding meanings.

That's because people often use words in unusual ways.

For instance, someone might say, 'That's a different kettle of fish!' What on earth do they mean?

People on the autism spectrum may find it harder to understand these everyday phrases.

Talking Point

What does 'a different kettle of fish' mean? Can you find out?

Other people can make things simpler for someone on the autism spectrum by saying what they mean and by explaining any strange phrases!

TIME FOR A PUZZLE!

Can you match these everyday phrases with what they really mean? Trace your finger along the coloured lines to find out.

Some of them don't seem to match their meanings at all, do they?

They're quite funny when you think about it!

Talking Point

If you enjoy this puzzle, you might like to know that there are two books written by Michael Barton, an adult on the autism spectrum, with lots more phrases like this explained. They are *It's Raining Cats and Dogs* and *A Different Kettle of Fish*, available from Jessica Kingsley Publishers.

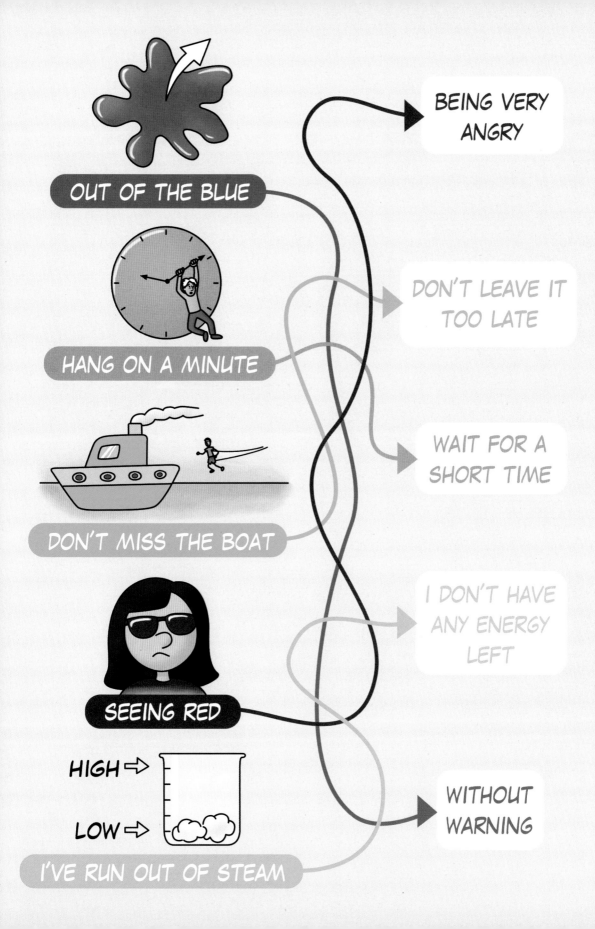

VANILLA ICE CREAM: TROUBLE WITH BEING A DETECTIVE

Sometimes it isn't just their words that tell us how people are feeling, but also how their faces and their bodies are moving.

Noticing little changes as a person moves their eyes and mouth is a bit like being a detective.

People who are not on the autism spectrum can usually guess how someone else is feeling just by looking at these tiny clues.

BEING A 'PEOPLE DETECTIVE'

Autistic people can have a lot of trouble understanding how someone is feeling unless a person tells them.

This is because they may not be able to decode the clues in faces and bodies quite as easily as other people.

They may even find it uncomfortable to look at someone's eyes.

In this book, we call being good at knowing what other people are thinking being a 'people detective'. Some people call this 'social skills'.

We can show this tricky trouble in our picture using a scoop of vanilla ice cream.

Just as with chocolate ice cream, this scoop can change its size. With a little help and practice, you can start to become a people detective.

Then that vanilla scoop starts to get smaller!

People can help by saying what they are feeling and why. Autistic people can't always guess, so this will be very useful.

BEING A PEOPLE DETECTIVE

TIME FOR A PUZZLE!

Look at these two pictures. Can you guess how the boy is feeling? Can you work out why he is feeling like that?

Being a people detective means looking for clues.

If you're puzzled about somebody's feelings, it's okay to ask them how they are feeling and why they are feeling that way, as long as you know them and they aren't a stranger.

STRAWBERRY ICE CREAM: STRAIGHT-LINE THINKING

Autistic people have what we call in this book 'straight-line thinking'. This means they like to know what is about to happen and they like things to stay the same.

They don't enjoy sudden changes.

When something unexpected happens, they can get upset, worried or scared.

Also, when something *doesn't* happen the way they *expect*, they can get upset.

In our ice-cream sundae, we show straight-line thinking as a scoop of strawberry ice cream. Everyone on the autism spectrum has it.

It causes people a lot of worry, because unfortunately life is full of little surprises. We can't stop unexpected things from happening, even when we try our very hardest to.

ZIG-ZAG THINKING

We can't stop the surprises that happen to us in life.

But we can help our thinking to bend a little.

When we hit those unwelcome changes, we can think of different ideas that might help us around the problem.

Guess what? The more we practise this, the better we become at it!

Instead of thinking in just straight lines, we start to be able to think in zig-zag lines, too!

Zig-zag thinking helps us to move around a problem more easily.

Just like these joggers in the park, we start to see ways we can move around problems so that they aren't such a worry to us any more.

Giving autistic people warnings when things are about to change is always a smart idea. What to expect, when to expect it and how long for...this information can make a person feel more comfortable, especially if it is written down.

TIME FOR A PUZZLE!

Let's play a game that involves zig-zag thinking!

Imagine that you want to go to the cinema, but it is closed when you get there. Can you think of different ways around the problem? Look at the picture. What could you do instead?

Talking Point

Our brains can only think of new ideas and solve problems when we feel nice and calm.

What helps you to keep calm?

TIME TO THINK...

Can you remember the three flavours of our ice-cream sundae and what part of autism each of them explain?

Talking Point

When autistic people are feeling nervous, worried or angry, those ice-cream scoops may look larger, because the things they have difficulty with seem to grow when they're unhappy. It's the same for all of us, isn't it?

But when people on the autism spectrum feel comfortable and calm, those ice-cream scoops may look smaller. When we panic, our bodies take over to protect us, just in case we are in danger. Being relaxed means that our brain gets to spend time thinking about words, people and problem-solving! Have you ever noticed that autism seems to affect people differently from day to day, or in different places? That's why.

What kinds of things do you think would make those ice-cream scoops bigger for you or someone you know? What kinds of things might make them smaller?

WHAT COMES NEXT?

The next things we are going to tell you about are common in autism.

Some people on the autism spectrum have these things and some don't.

They are the extras in our ice-cream sundae.

SENSORY DIFFERENCES

Have you ever felt so cold or hungry that you can't think clearly?

When your body is not comfortable, you can find it hard to think!

Lights, sounds, smells and even the way that something feels against their skin may be uncomfortable for someone on the autism spectrum.

For example, what other people hear as quiet sounds may sound much louder to them. Some lights might seem brighter.

Some materials might feel extra scratchy.

An autistic person may not realize that these things feel different for them.

In this book, we call these types of differences 'sensory differences'.

CHOCOLATE SAUCE: SENSORY DIFFERENCES

So how do these 'sensory differences' look on our ice-cream sundae?

Think of sensory differences as some runny chocolate sauce.

If you've ever tried to pour chocolate sauce on ice cream, sometimes it covers all the ice cream. You can't even see the ice cream – all you can see is chocolate sauce!

In autism, 'sensory differences' can get in the way, just like our chocolate sauce.

None of us can think very well when our bodies don't feel comfortable. If you are on the autism spectrum and you're uncomfortable because of 'sensory differences', it's harder than usual to deal with that other tricky stuff.

Tricky troubles with words may be more difficult.

Being a people detective may seem harder than ever.

Zig-zag thinking may seem impossible!

Once those uncomfortable things are taken away, it's much easier to help a person on the autism spectrum.

Brains think better when bodies are comfortable!

TIME FOR A PUZZLE!

Have a look at this picture. What can you see that might make an unexpected sound?

Talking Point

Would any of the sounds in the picture make you uncomfortable? Sometimes even the thought of a sound that could happen can make a person with sensory differences feel like running away. Can you see anything that might be about to make a loud sound?

THE WAFER: FEELINGS WE CAN SEE

Some people can hide their bigger feelings inside their bodies and not show what they are feeling.

Many autistic people find that nearly impossible. Their bodies move, or they shout out loud.

That's because big feelings build up quickly inside them and soon become too big for them to hide.

This is why autistic people sometimes flap their arms or hands when they're excited.

In our autism sundae, easy-to-see feelings are shown with a wafer that goes with our ice cream.

Many autistic people do not hide their feelings and this is a lovely part of who they are.

If you struggle to keep yourself calm when you want to, this is something we call self-regulation.

EASY-TO-SEE
FEELINGS

MELTED ICE CREAM: 'MELTDOWNS'

When lots of things are happening around an autistic person and it gets too much, they can experience what we sometimes call 'overload'.

That's when they may find it hard to keep all the angry and upset feelings inside their bodies.

They might have big outbursts, sometimes called 'meltdowns', which they later feel sorry about.

Once they're upset, it can take a while for an autistic person to calm themselves down.

That's not their fault – it's just how their brains work.

The great news is that autistic people can *learn* ways to make themselves feel calmer. They can get much better at stopping these big feelings from getting so big that they take over!

Talking Point

What things make you feel happy and calm when you're upset? It's a good idea to think of these things when you are feeling okay, so that friends and family know how they can help you when you sometimes feel a bit sad.

If other people understand the ingredients that make our ice-cream sundae, they will be able to help if someone starts to get upset.

MELTDOWNS

SPRINKLES: THE BEST BITS!

People on the autism spectrum have different kinds of brains.

Because they find it easier to learn by looking rather than listening, autistic people can often spot the little things the rest of us don't notice.

That 'straight-line' thinking means that once they start doing something they like, they don't give up or get tired easily.

Because of this, lots of autistic people can become quite expert at the things they like to do.

They can also be very patient.

And they can have extremely good memories.

Talking Point

What do you like doing most? Is there a subject you know a lot about?

When new information is linked to familiar topics, autistic people find it much easier to learn. Find ways of using favourite topics to practise new skills.

TIME FOR A PUZZLE!

Ask your friends and family what their 'sprinkles' are. What are they good at? What do they love doing? Are they good at the same things as you or different things?

CHERRY: A SPECIAL TALENT

Some autistic people have really special skills.

Because their brains aren't using up a lot of energy with 'people detective' work, all that energy goes into other parts of their brains. Because of this, some people on the autism spectrum are unusually talented.

When someone on the autism spectrum is especially gifted, our ice-cream sundae has a cherry on top!

Today, famous people on the autism spectrum include Satoshi Tajiri, the inventor of Pokémon. His attention to detail meant that he had the patience to develop hundreds of characters.

Talking Point

See if you can find Willard Wigan and Stephen Wiltshire on the internet. They are both on the autism spectrum, but what special skills are they famous for? Do you like their work? We do!

SPECIAL
SKILLS

IT'S NEARLY TIME TO GO!

We hope you've enjoyed our ice-cream sundae!

Thank you for reading this book.

We are almost finished, but...

DRAW YOUR OWN ICE-CREAM SUNDAE

...there's one last thing.

Would you like to draw your own ice-cream sundae?

Can you remember what each flavour means?

Does your own ice-cream sundae have chocolate sauce? Or maybe you'd like a different sauce!

How about sprinkles?

You might like to colour in this ice-cream sundae. Or you may prefer to draw your own.

Maybe you think it's perfect in black and white, just the way it is.

We'll let you decide.

USING THIS BOOK:
FOR PARENTS AND TEACHERS

For autistic children, it's vital that they don't feel silly or wrong; that they understand that certain brains just happen to be built differently.

The ice-cream sundae helps to explain autism in a neutral way, without negative judgement on any aspect of it.

For siblings and peers, understanding autism leads to acceptance and tolerance. For those on the autism spectrum, it leads to self-awareness and confidence.

We wrote this book for all children – not just those on the autism spectrum.

The beauty of the ice-cream sundae is that it isn't describing *one* person's autism – that person may not be at all like your child! It describes everybody's autism, and their job is to select the ingredients that describe them, their classmate or family member.

For teachers, groups and clubs, we suggest you use this book to guide you through a fun practical session on autism, making ice-cream sundaes with your class. Studies show that peers who have just a little understanding are much more likely to befriend and support autistic classmates.

Thank you for buying this book. Have fun reading and sharing it!

FOR PARENTS

Introducing autism to your child or their siblings shouldn't be just one conversation. You can start in a simple way, by using this book, and then develop your explanations over time. It also makes more sense to talk about autism to your children 'on the go', so that their understanding builds almost without them realizing.

To do this, if they come across something that causes them difficulty because of their autism, you can say, 'Do you remember the ice-cream sundae book? Well, you're struggling with this because it's part of autism. But the good news is that we can help you with it...' We always like to point out that autism has both advantages and disadvantages, so it might be nice to point out at the same time what your child is good at because of their autism. This might be something like having more patience with a subject than other children, or knowing a topic really well. Always point out the 'sprinkles'!

To help your conversations develop as your child gets older, you may like to start introducing the professional terminology for what we've explained in the pages of this book:

- Chocolate ice cream: Speech and language
- Vanilla ice cream: Social skills
- Strawberry ice cream: Rigidity of thought
- Chocolate sauce: Sensory differences, or sensory processing disorder (SPD)
- Wafer: Self-regulation

FOR TEACHERS

Class Activities

1. If you are making an ice-cream sundae with the class, demonstrate your own first and then let them do theirs, remembering which characteristic they are adding as they go. When telling pupils about ice-cream scoops, it helps to point out all the factors that influence their size: not only someone's autism, but their environment and how anxious they are. Over time and with some help in each area of difficulty, the scoop sizes can reduce quite a lot.

2. Draw your own autism sundae.

3. Try using sarcasm and asking students to analyse how they spotted it. When people don't say exactly what they mean, what can we do to help an autistic person?

4. Sensory differences: You can ask students to complete a quiz but distract them with noisy music. Ask them to imagine trying to do homework while sitting in a disco. Let them know that this is how a noisy classroom can feel to an autistic child.

5. Show the pupils work by the artist Stephen Wiltshire and the sculptor Willard Wigan. It's important that children understand that difference doesn't always mean disability.

THE BACKGROUND

In 2013, *AuKids* magazine, a magazine for parents and carers of children on the autism spectrum, published an article titled 'The Autism Sundae Dessert (or ASD to some)'.

The *AuKids* editors (that's us!) felt that the complexity of autism meant that it was never explained in a simple enough way for families to share.

We felt that the traditional term 'triad of impairments' was neither a complete nor a positive way of describing autism to people new to the condition. It made it more difficult for parents to find positive language when it came to explaining autism to their children.

So we created a modern definition that could show autism as a difference rather than a disability – and as a condition that evolves over time rather than remaining static.

Readers started asking for copies of the article to bring to support groups and training. We produced posters of it, and we began to make the dessert in live demonstrations during training sessions to help people remember it.

When we were asked to demonstrate the sundae for a group of Girl Guides, we set about creating the sort of session that could be used by any teacher to develop autism awareness.

The ice-cream sundae has become so popular that we decided to develop this book, for children on the autism spectrum and their family and friends.

We hope you will make it part of your autism kit and use it to help children understand what autism is and how it affects people.

ABOUT THE ILLUSTRATOR

J.C. Perry is the graphic designer behind *AuKids* magazine,
a social enterprise founded by this book's co-authors in 2008.
As well as being an illustrator, she is also an award-winning 2D
and 3D animator. She and her husband, Paul, own Periscope
Studios in Delph, Lancashire. Her book illustrations can be
viewed at www.jcperry.info.

ACKNOWLEDGEMENTS

We'd like to say a big 'thanks' to all of our magazine readers,
who gave us such great feedback on the 'Autism Sundae'
and encouraged us to bring the idea to the wider public.

Thanks also to our family and friends who have given us
so much encouragement with *AuKids* magazine and with
this project.

Finally, thanks to Debby's twin sons, Bobby and Alec, and
Tori's son, Remy, who inspire us to make the world a better
place for others, even if our contribution is just a small one.

Debby Elley and Tori Houghton